SUCCEEDING IN THE REAL WORLD

What School WON'T Teach You

Hoan Do

Succeeding in the Real World: What School WON'T Teach You

Send inquiries to:

Hoan Do

Hoan Do Companies, LLC

1911 SW Campus Drive, Suite #572

Federal Way, WA 98023

Telephone: 206.257.9515

www.succeedingintherealworld.com

ISBN: 978-1-890427-12-2

Library of Congress — applied for 2009

Editor: Shannon Evans — www.bainbridgebusinesspress.com

Cover Design & Typesetting: www.fusioncw.com

Every attempt has been made to source all quotes properly.

Printed in San Francisco

1st Edition

For Additional Copies visit:

www.succeedingintherealworld.com

PRAISE FOR
SUCCEEDING IN THE REAL WORLD

"At the beginning of my senior year, I was stressed out about finding a job after college. After speaking with you during 1st semester, I took your advice that is shared in your book and applied it. Two months later, I landed my dream job in General Electric's prestigious Financial Management Program! I was able to enjoy the rest of my senior year with peace and confidence."

~ Nikhil Jacob, Student, Pepperdine University

"Succeeding in the Real World is a practical guide to life after college. All college students should read it so they will learn what the university system will not teach them. From overcoming fear to changing your attitude, and prioritizing your goals, Hoan Do shows college students how to succeed. As a former college professor, I would have recommended this book to my own students."

~ Tyler R. Tichelaar, Ph.D. and author of The Marquette Trilogy

3

"I have benefited greatly from all of Hoan's insight. Every student and recent graduate needs to read this book because it shares real solutions for the real world challenges that every young person encounters."

~ Brendan Groves, Law Student, Yale University

"Transitioning from school to the real world was a huge culture shock for me. I was not prepared. Adjusting to life without my close friends, professors and mentors nearby was challenging. You have helped me to get more clarity in what I want to do with my life by asking me questions that no one has ever asked me. Because of the information that you share in Succeeding in the Real World, I am more confident and now have more direction in my life."

~ Stephanie Doe, College Graduate and Intern, International Justice Mission

"It's refreshing to hear from someone I can relate to and who knows what I am going through. Your advice has helped me to deal with the many challenges I have come across in the real world."

~ Brandon Abang, Student, University of Washington

ACKNOWLEDGEMENTS

This book and all that has happened in my life would not have been possible if it were not for the many people who have influenced my life.

To Mom and Dad, Thi and Van: Thank you for all the sacrifices you have made for me throughout my life. You have supported me in all of my dreams and endeavors even if you didn't agree. I would not be the person I am today if it were not for the two of you. Thank you for being an inspiration in my life. I could not have asked for more loving and caring parents.

To my brother Hoc: You have been an amazing brother and role model for me throughout my entire life. Thanks for always believing in me even when I didn't believe in myself and for always having my back.

To my high school math teacher, Ms. Joyce Baker: Thank you for the generosity, care and attention that you provided for your students. Our school system would be much greater if there were more teachers like you.

To my high school wrestling coach, Mike Bressler: You taught me how important mental toughness is for success. I carry this concept with me to this day.

To Mike Costache and Alexis Bonnell: Your class provided me with the essential skills to succeed in life. Both of you inspired me through your lives and actions. You showed me that age should not be a factor to hold me back from reaching my goals in life.

To Art Mortell: Thank you for taking me under your wing as a seventeen year old kid. Your advice and guidance has been priceless.

To Ricky Sohal: Thank you for opening up my eyes to an entirely different world. Much of what I have been able to do and accomplish in life is because of your influence.

To Mandy Pratt: You have supported and advised me through the most difficult times in my life. You have had a profound impact on my life and I thank you.

To Bart Smith: Thank you for reinforcing the fact that I needed to write a book and for being one cool guy.

To my 'boys' Nikhil, Chris and Jordan: I am very lucky to have such amazing and encouraging friends.

To Mike Hutchison: Thank you for all of your guidance and for always checking up on me.

To Barry Garapedian: Uncle Barry, you always help me put life into perspective when I am in a funk. You always inspire me to take life to the next level.

To Patrick Snow: This book would have never happened if it were not for you. I want to thank you for giving a talk back when I was a high school junior, thank you for giving me your book, and thank you for continuously reminding me that I need to write a book.

To Shannon Evans: This book not have happened if it wasn't for your patience with me. Thank you.

To Tony Robbins: Your work has profoundly impacted my life in ways you could never imagine. Thank you for sharing your gift to the world.

CONTENTS

SUCCEEDING IN THE REAL WORLD
WHAT SCHOOL WON'T TEACH YOU
INTRODUCTION

While in school I often sat in classes wondering "When am I ever going to use this information in my life?" I would ask myself, "Why don't we ever learn about things that will actually help us to succeed in the real world?"

Instead of learning about the important things that would help me to succeed in life, like how to get through challenging times, how to discover my passions, how to set and achieve goals, how to make and manage my money or how to land a job after school, I learned information that did not immediately apply to my life like mathematical equations, scientific formulas and random facts about foreign countries.

As a freshman in college, I would hear horror stories from students who had graduated and were now in the real world. They said that working full time, paying bills and living outside of the academic environment was a culture shock. They complained that their classes did not teach them the important lessons on how to adjust to life after college. They also told me that college was going to be the best four years of my life so enjoy myself while I can because after I graduated it was not going to be as fun.

After hearing all of this, I was definitely not looking forward to leaving the safe and cozy setting of school to enter into the unpredictable and scary real world. So I made a decision that I didn't want to end up like the college graduates who were struggling to survive in the real world. I figured that if I wasn't learning everything I needed to know from school, then I would take it upon myself to learn the practical skills that would help me to thrive in the real world.

There were many late nights where I stayed up and read books on personal and professional growth. I spent my weekends traveling around the country attending seminars on leadership and business. I met and learned from top experts from around the world in communications, personal finance and goal setting. And most importantly, I went out and put myself into real life situations from dealing with the challenges of starting a company to attending business functions and interacting with professionals who were twice my age.

It has been two years now since my college graduation and life could not be better. I love what I do, I meet great people every day and I have an amazing group of friends. With that said, I will admit that during my transition from academic life to real life I made a ton of mistakes, came across many challenging situations and experienced lots of adversity. I believe though that because of the practical knowledge I learned from putting myself into real world situations while in school, I equipped myself to have a smoother transition and was better able to handle the life situations that came after college.

I wrote this book because I wished I had something like the advice I am presenting here when I was in school. I believe that the ideas and advice from this book can help you because I am a fellow young person like you who has gone through what you will soon experience when you graduate. I figured that I could help keep you from making the mistakes I have made, and that you can learn from my experiences.

Now I want to make it clear that I don't know everything and that this book does not have all of life's answers. Every day I learn something new about me and about life.

In *Succeeding in the Real World*, I address the most commonly asked questions from students when it comes to graduating and entering into a new chapter in their lives after college.

- What is life like after college?
- How do I find and land a job in the career I want?
- What is my social life going to be like post-graduation?
- How will I balance my life with work, family, and friends?
- How will I manage the stresses and challenges of life?
- What if I get a job I hate?
- How am I going to pay off school loans and credit card debts?
- What am I passionate about?
- What am I going to do with my life?

Now don't worry; this is not like the textbooks you read for class. (Well that's assuming you actually read your textbooks from class.....) This book is rather a guide for life after college. It is an easy and fun read with straight forward advice that actually relates to your life. The purpose of this book is to help you become aware of what you can expect after graduation and to equip you with ideas, tools and practical skills to succeed in the real world.

Before you begin reading, here are a few tips you will want to know to get the most out of this book:

Have an open mind. As you read, you will learn new ideas, perspectives and concepts. Be willing to try to apply the new information you take away.

Take notes. Keep a pen and journal handy because you will be learning relevant and useful information that applies to your life. You will want to write down these awesome ideas because you will find yourself reflecting back and using them often.

Apply what you learn. There is a saying that knowledge is power. I disagree. Applied knowledge is power. I believe the best way to learn is by doing. Throughout each chapter, you will see exercises called, Turning Knowledge into Action. The purpose of these exercises is to help you apply great ideas now so they will have a positive impact on your life today rather than having them just be a great idea that you read about.

Read this book more than once. *Succeeding in the Real World* is not meant to be read once and then thrown on the bookshelf to collect dust. After reading this book once, you will realize a lot of great information is in it. You won't be able to apply everything that you learn after reading the book once so by reading sections of *Succeeding in the Real World* over and over again you will gain a better understanding of the information and take away new ideas and practical advice each time that will help you to succeed in your new life. This book may be exactly what you have been looking for. As you read each page, you will begin to feel more confident as you prepare to graduate and begin your life after college.

Whether you are a current student or a recent graduate, I know you can succeed in the real world and in life because I believe in you.

As you prepare for this next stage in your life, I want you to know I am here for you.

Here's to your Success in the Real World!

Your Friend,

Hoan Do

Hoan Do

CHAPTER I:

ATTITUDE – THE DIFFERENCE BETWEEN SURVIVING AND THRIVING

"The greatest discovery of my generation is that a human being can alter his life by altering his attitudes of mind."

~ William James, Philosopher and Psychologist

Do you know of people who have graduated and are having difficult time transitioning from academic life to 'real' life? They are the ones who complain about how they hate life outside of school? Do you know of other people who have graduated but are having a completely different experience? In the midst of the challenges, they are doing fairly well and enjoying themselves. Have you ever wondered, "What is the difference between those two groups of people? How is it that one group can struggle to survive while the other is enjoying life and thriving?"

THE SMALL THING THAT MAKES A BIG DIFFERENCE

While I was in school, I had many friends who had graduated and struggled in the real world. Often they would complain about how they disliked their jobs and how hard life was with all the responsibilities of being an adult. After hearing all of their complaining, I began to believe the real world wasn't as great as I thought it would be, until I met two young successful college alumnus who came back to teach a course at our school. One of the graduates was an entrepreneur who owned a handful of companies and had a vision of someday becoming the U.S. ambassador to Romania. The other graduate was a triple major and one of the youngest chief marketing officers in her industry. After meeting both of these former students, I was amazed by their achievements and their positive outlook on life. I thought to myself, "What is the difference between them and the people I know?" How were they thriving while my friends were struggling to survive? Did they have higher GPA's? Was it that they graduated with a specific degree? As I spent more time with them, I realized it was none of those reasons; their success in the real world was due to having the "right" attitude.

HAVING THE "RIGHT" ATTITUDE

Now don't worry. I'm not here to tell you that if you have a positive mental attitude you will succeed in life. You have probably heard that from so many people that you are sick and tired of hearing that by now. I believe being positive is important, but having the "right" attitude means having the ability to see a situation as it is, not worse than it is and potentially seeing it better than what it is currently.

With the current job market, I know that many students are worried about finding a place to work after college. Right now in the United States, the unemployment rate is about 10%. When people hear this, they begin to think it is the end of the world. They think no companies are hiring and finding a job will be nearly impossible. They make the situation worse than it actually is. Having this attitude or perspective does not help you go out and find work. The reality is, companies are still hiring; they are just being more selective. Job candidates now have to refine their skills and show employers they have the experience and skills that companies are looking for when hiring.

It is important to understand that your attitude affects your actions and your actions affect the results in your life. In the example above, if you see that the job market is bleak and that finding a job is impossible, you more than likely won't put forth 100% effort to find a job. If you choose to take the perspective that companies are still hiring, but that they are being more selective, you will feel more hopeful and therefore put more effort into finding and landing a position with a company.

I know you may be thinking right now that having the "right" attitude sounds a lot easier said than done, and I agree with you. What I want you to know is that having the "right" attitude is something you can learn and develop through practice. First though, you have to have a good understanding of what affects your attitude.

WHAT DO YOU BELIEVE?

What is a belief? Have you ever really pondered that question? A belief seems like something that is out there and abstract. All a belief is really is a feeling. It's a feeling of certainty or confidence that you have about something. For example I can ask, "Do you believe or are you confident that you can tie your shoe?" Hopefully you will say yes; however, if I ask, "Do you believe you know what you want to do with your life?" you may be less certain and would answer with less confidence.

Our beliefs are important because they affect our attitudes and how we view things in life, which then impacts our actions and then our results that we get in life.

Beliefs -> Attitude -> Actions -> Results

"How we think shows through in how we act."

~ Dr. David Schwartz, Author

Imagine you hear a story about a child being raised up in a poor and drug addicted family. By the age of fifteen, she is left homeless to live on the streets because her mother died due to AIDS and her father abandoned her. What would you think the future would hold for this young girl? Would you think that she would become a drug addict, perhaps involved in criminal activity? Would you be surprised if I told you that with little formal high school education, Liz Murray won a scholarship from the New York Times for a full ride to Harvard? A movie was created about this incredible young woman called Homeless to Harvard, and she now speaks all around the world to share her inspiring story.

Liz Murray's story is a perfect example of how our beliefs affect our lives. Can you imagine going through all that she had to go through at such a young age? Most people in her situation probably would give up or just believe that their lives would always be miserable. Rather than believing the challenges she had to go through would hold her back, she believed they would help her to succeed and to inspire others. It was this belief that kept her going during those tough times.

> *"10% of life is made up of what happens to you;*
> *90 % of life is decided by how you react to it."*
> *~ Stephen Covey, Best Selling Author and Speaker*

What is important to understand is that your beliefs can serve and help you, or they can paralyze and sabotage you. The key is to notice and reject the beliefs that are not helping you and to choose to embrace the beliefs that do.

WHERE DO OUR BELIEFS COME FROM?

Our beliefs come from two different sources:

- Other People

  This can range from your parents, friends and people you run into throughout life. When I was growing up, my parents always taught me the importance of getting good grades, going to college and getting a good job. Because of my parents' influence, I studied hard, went to college, and got a good job.

- Life Experiences

   Your personal experiences affect your beliefs. Have you ever had to do a presentation in front of a group of people? Public speaking is considered the number one fear for most people. Many people have a bad first experience and from that they believe they are not good at public speaking or that it is too hard.

HOW TO HAVE THE "RIGHT" ATTITUDE WHEN THINGS GO WRONG

   Developing the "right" attitude is something that is learned and worked at over time. Below are three tips that will help you develop the "right" attitude:

   1. *Whenever you feel like you have a negative outlook or can only see a situation one way, ask yourself, "What else can this mean?"*

   Asking this question will help you to focus on the positive or other side of a situation. This will then provide you with the possibility that things can get better.

   2. *Pay close attention to what and whom you listen to.*

   Your mind is like a garden. In your garden, there are flowers and weeds. Flowers represent positive thoughts; the weeds represent negative, destructive thoughts. In every garden as in life, weeds (self doubters, negative news, etc.) will pop up and need to be pulled, or they will take over. Make sure you stand guard to what you allow yourself to believe. Make sure you don't listen to those who are negative about life. If you wanted to pass a class, would you get advice from someone who was failing? Of course not. It's the same with life. Don't take advice from people who are struggling in the real world.

   3. *Meet and spend time with successful people.*

   This will give you first-hand experience of the value of having the "right" attitude. Their positive attitudes will rub off on you.

MOVING OUT OF SURVIVAL MODE

To move out of the one-track view that the real world is horrific and overwhelming, I advise every student to get a taste of the real world while still in school. This will help you to prepare yourself physically and mentally when making the transition to the real world.

Preparing to make that leap into the real world after graduation is like preparing for a test. You wouldn't go into an exam without any preparation would you? Let me take that back, you shouldn't go into an exam without preparation. When you do go unprepared, what is often the result? Usually a poor performance. To get a taste of the real world get a job with a company where you will do real life work, manage your own finances, and attend events with people who are older than you to help build your interpersonal skills. By doing activities like this, it will help you see what it will be like when you do leave school and help you have a smoother transition.

TURNING KNOWLEDGE INTO ACTION

1. What is your attitude about what life will be like after school? Is your view one sided? Are you seeing it worse than it actually is?

_____

_____

_____

2. What are your current beliefs around the real world? Do you believe that college will be the best four years of your life? Do you believe that life after college will be stressful and no longer fun?

_____

_____

_____

3. Where do most of your beliefs come from?

_____

_____

_____

4. What can you do today to prepare yourself for the real world? (i.e. Apply for an internship, meet with a mentor to get advice, etc.)

_____

_____

_____

TAKE-AWAYS

- The difference between people who struggle to survive and people who thrive in the real world is not what their GPA's were in school, what they majored in or the schools they graduated from; it comes to down to their attitude.

- Having the "right" attitude helps you to see a situation as it is, not worse than it is. Attitude is a learned skill.

- Your beliefs affect your attitude, which impacts the actions you take and the results you get in life.

- Your beliefs are influenced by other people and your own personal experiences. To develop the "right" attitude, when confronted by a challenge ask yourself, "What else can this mean?" In addition, pay careful attention to whom you listen to or get advice from, and spend time learning from successful people.

- To get out of survival mode, go out and decide to prepare yourself for life after college by putting yourself in the real world now. Get a job where you would have responsibilities like a regular employee, live in your own place, etc.

CHAPTER 2:

GOALS: GETTING FROM WHERE YOU ARE TO WHERE YOU WANT TO BE

"The best way you can predict your future is to create it."

~ Stephen Covey, Best Selling Author and Speaker

In school you have nearly everything laid out for you, from your meals in the cafeteria to the classes you need to take to graduate. The real world is nothing like that. In life there is no study guide or step-by-step instructions showing you what you need to do to succeed or how to pass the tests that life gives you. In the real world, you are left to create your own plan for your life. This can be a bit overwhelming since there was always a clear path to follow while in school and now there is not. This can also be exciting because now you get to decide what you want to do, what you want to learn and experience. A big question is where do I start? You start with creating goals.

GOALS, HOW IMPORTANT CAN THEY REALLY BE?

Imagine you and your friends decide to go camping. As you jump onto the freeway, you realize you have no idea how to get to the camp-site, so what do you do? You ask for directions, or you get a map to help guide you in the right direction. Goals are like maps; they help you get from point A (where you are) to point B (where you want to be). Without goals, you could start going in the wrong direction and end up never reaching your final destination. That's what many college students are doing today. They leave school without a map of what they want and where they want to go, so they get frustrated and often end up working at a job they hate. No wonder so many graduates have bitter experiences with life after college. Without goals, you are left in the passenger's seat with no control of where you will go. By having goals, you put yourself firmly in the driver's seat of your life.

SO WHERE DO I BEGIN?

At all the leadership classes and conferences I attended, there were so many different ways to create and achieve goals. I realized that what worked best was to keep things simple. Whenever I am setting goals for myself, I just answer these three simple questions:

1. What do you want?
2. Why do you want it?
3. When do you want to achieve it (date)?

WHAT DO YOU WANT?

When was the last time you sat down and asked, "What do I really want?" It's easy to fall into a day-to-day routine where we forget to think about what is important to us. Would you like to go backpacking in Europe? Run a marathon? Start your own company? Get a brand new car? Whatever you want to have, do or be, it has to excite you. When thinking about what you want and your goals in life, dream big like when you were a kid. Imagine if you could achieve and do anything; if you could not fail, what would you want?

"Everything you can imagine is real."

~ Pablo Picasso, Artist

Don't worry about how you are going to achieve it. It doesn't matter because every great idea or accomplishment began as a thought. I am giving you permission to be impractical. Make a decision not to be like the many people who graduate and lose sight of their dreams because of the challenges they run into in the real world.

WHY DO YOU WANT IT?

After you decide what you want, the next question to ask is, "Why do I want it?" One of the biggest reasons why most people don't get where they want to be in life is because they don't know why they want it in the first place. A good example of this is choosing a major in college. A goal in college is deciding upon a major. It is not unusual to change one's major multiple times throughout a college career. Students accomplish the goal of choosing a major when they understand why they like one area of study over another.

Your 'why' or your purpose is what keeps you motivated to achieve your goals. Knowing the reasons why you want to achieve a goal will help you get through the many times when you feel unmotivated and want to give up.

WHEN DO YOU WANT TO ACHIEVE IT (DATE)?

Do you know people who have said, "Someday, I will…." When do they actually do it? Having a date for when you want to accomplish a goal is important because without it, the goal will never happen.

When you are assigned a major paper to be written and completed at the end of the semester, when do you begin working on it? Are you diligent enough to start the paper right away and finish early? If so I applaud you. Most students take it easy until a couple of weeks or even days before the paper is due. If you never had a deadline, then the paper would never get done. The same is true with a goal.

"A goal is a dream with a deadline."

~ Napoleon Hill, Business Thinker and Author

COMMITMENT

"Hoan, I want to be successful, I want to be financially well off, and I want to be happy in life." I meet many people who want a lot of things in life. What I have learned is that we don't get what we want. We get what we are committed to achieving.

Is commitment to your goal waking up an extra hour earlier to exercise? Is it not going out on Friday nights to save money, or is it working on Saturdays to make some extra money? Writing this book was not an easy process. It took me over a year and a half to take this book from being an idea to making it into print. There were many weekends where I woke up early and stayed up late. There were plenty of weekends where I didn't hang out with friends to get this book done.

A mentor of mine shared with me a great example to illustrate how you have to stay committed to reaching your goals. Imagine right now that you are standing in a line waiting for food. At the end of the line, you can see every possible type of food. There is no cutting, so the only way to get food is to start at the back of the line. You're waiting in line, but it feels as if you are moving an inch every half hour. You decide that it's taking too long so you get out of line. You begin to walk out of the cafeteria, but in the back of your mind, a little voice says to you, "Feed me. I'm hungry." You decide to return to the cafeteria to get some food. The only thing is that you can't go back to your old spot; you have to begin at the back of the line. As you wait again in line, you doubt whether it was a good decision because it's taking too long. You then decide it's not worth it, so after moving a couple feet, you get out of line again. This is a metaphor for life. Many people want to reach the end of the line to achieve the goals they have set; however, few are committed and willing to put in the time and effort it takes to get to the front.

24

MEASURING YOUR PROGRESS

Now that you are doing something every day to move toward your goals, make sure you measure your progress. What this will do is help you to know whether you are on track. If you are not, then you know you have to change your approach or what you are doing to reach your goals.

Let me give you an example. Let's say that your goal is to move into your own apartment by the end of next year. To make this happen, you know that you have to save $1,200 to cover the security deposit and the first month's rent. So you make a plan to save $200 a month for the next six months. Four months pass by, and you look at your bank account, and you notice that you saved a total of $600. Since you measured your progress, you realize that after four months, you should have saved a total of $800 (4 months X $200). You are $200 off because of the new clothes you bought at the mall. Because you measured your progress, you know you will be off by $200 at the end of six months, so for the next two months you save $300 each month to make up for your spending spree; now you know you will reach your goal.

SETTING YOURSELF UP TO WIN

As you work toward achieving your goals, you will run into challenges and setbacks. There will be times where you will get distracted and times when you may want to give up. The key is to set yourself up to win. You must put things in place that help you to get through the tough times. Below are a few ideas that will help keep you on track for reaching your goals.

1. *Review your goals daily*

A big reason why many people never achieve their New Year's resolutions is because they wait until the following year to see if they accomplished them. Take a moment every day to review your goals. This will help you to re-focus and stay on track. A great time to review your goals is in the morning or at night before bed. As you review your goals, imagine yourself as if you have already accomplished your goals. Feel the way that you would be feeling; say to yourself the things that you would be saying if your goals were already reality. See yourself already having accomplished your goals.

2. *Do something every day to move toward your goal*

There is a great saying by Keith Cunningham, "Ordinary things done consistently produce extraordinary results." Rather than doing everything in one day, like when cramming for a test, do something every day to move you closer to achieving your goal.

3. *Accountability*

Share your dreams and ambitions with others. By sharing, you put yourself in a position where you are not only succeeding for yourself but for others. It puts positive pressure on you to follow through on what you said you are going to do. Find other people who have the same goals and help support each other.

4. *Celebrate Along the Way*

As you move closer to completing your goals, make sure you celebrate along the way. Give yourself a pat on the back for making progress; we never give ourselves enough credit. Reward yourself for taking major steps in the direction of the goals you set for yourself. Buy yourself that new CD you wanted or take a break and hang out with friends for the weekend. By celebrating along the way, you will have more fun as you move closer to achieving your goals. The more fun you have, the more likely you are to follow through and continue what you are doing.

5. *Create a Goal Collage*

This is a fun process that will help you become more engaged and make your goals more real. Cut out pictures, images and phrases from magazines, newspapers, etc. representing the things you want to have or achieve. If your goal was to move to New York to live and work after you graduate, you could cut out a picture of Broadway and clip out words like the Big Apple. After you make your collage, put it where you can see it on a daily basis. My goal collage is in my day planner, and I look at it every morning and night. Having a goal collage is one of the best things you can do to help you remain focused and excited in accomplishing your goals.

WHAT IF I DON'T ACHIEVE MY GOAL?

There will be times throughout your life where you don't exactly reach the goal you set for yourself. It doesn't mean you failed; it just means you didn't achieve your goal.

You might be wondering, "What's the point of having goals if you don't accomplish them?" The purpose of a goal is to stretch you, to help you do what you wouldn't ordinarily do and in doing so, it helps you to grow and become a better person. When you set your eyes on something you really want, it usually forces you to do something out of your comfort zone. And whether you reach your goal or not, you will learn new skills and have new experiences.

John Wooden, legendary UCLA basketball coach, is considered the greatest college basketball coach of all time. In sixteen years, he and his teams won over ten national championships. An interviewer asked him, "What is the secret to your success?" He replied, "To never have my players focus on winning but rather giving their all." He told his players that there will be times when you may play a team that is not as good as you, and you will easily outscore them. There will also be times where you will play a team that is far more skilled, and they will have more points at the end of the game. What determines whether you win is not the points on the board, but rather how much better you have become. Outscoring a team that is not good won't make you better. Playing a team that is more skilled and playing every second that you are on the floor with everything you have will make you a better player. If you can honestly say that you left everything out on the court, then you don't have to look at the scoreboard to see if you won; you can walk away knowing you are a winner.

I share this story with you because you may fall short of achieving your goal, but it doesn't mean that you lost. If you gave it your all and you did things you ordinarily would not have done, then you can walk away knowing you are a winner. The reward of achieving a goal really isn't what you achieved, but rather what you have learned and who you become in the process.

TURNING KNOWLEDGE INTO ACTION

1. What is something you have always wanted to do, be or have? (Remember your goal must EXCITE YOU!!)

_____

_____

_____

2. Why is this goal so important to you? How will achieving this goal make you feel? What will it mean to you to accomplish this goal? What will you say to yourself? What is going to pull you through when the going gets tough?

_____

_____

_____

3. When do you want to achieve it? (Example: October 17 of this year?)

_____

_____

_____

4. What are you willing to give in return? What sacrifices are you willing to make to get to where you want or need to be? Remember people don't get what they want in life; they get what they are committed to achieving.

_____

_____

5. What will you need to do to accomplish what you want? Make a list of things you can do today to move you closer toward your goals.

_____

_____

_____

TAKE-AWAYS

- There are no clear-cut instructions or outlines to follow to succeed in the real world.
- Having goals is like having a map. They will help you to get from where you are to where you want to be. Put yourself in the driver's seat of your life by having goals.
- To start, begin by asking yourself what do you want? Why do you want it, and when do you want to achieve it by?
- You don't get what you want; you get what you are committed to achieving.
- Measure your Progress – This will help you to know whether you are on track or whether you need to change your approach.
- Set Yourself Up to Win – Review your goals daily, do something every day to move closer to your goals, share your dreams with others, celebrate your progress and create a vision board to help make your goals more real.
- If you don't achieve your goal, you didn't fail or lose. The purpose of a goal is to help you to grow and to become a better person. If you gave it your all, you can walk away knowing you are a winner.

CHAPTER 3:

TIME MANAGEMENT - THE BALANCING ACT

"Time = life; therefore, waste your time and waste of your

life, or master your time and master your life."

~ Alan Lakein, Author and Time Management Expert

Do you ever feel overwhelmed? Have you ever felt that there is just too much to do and not enough time in the day? I know how you feel. In college you have to keep up with classes, work and of course squeeze in some time to have a social life and fun. After graduating you begin your full time career and explore the adventures that come with life after college.

You are probably thinking, "Will this fast pace ever slow down?" It is possible to have balance in life where you still get things done and also have fun? The answer is yes but it is just going to take a shift in the way that you think and in what you do (your approach).

THERE ARE ONLY 24 HOURS IN A DAY

Have you ever fallen in the trap of saying to yourself that there is just not enough time in the day? Let's get something straight, there are only 24 hours in a day, no more, no less. Everybody has the same 24 hours each and every day. Rather than wishing that there was more time in a day to do everything, it comes down to making better choices of how you spend your time and what you spend your time doing.

WHAT ARE YOU UP TO?

Have you ever sat down and asked yourself, "What am I involved in?" Today I see that many people can't keep track of all the things that they do. If you ever feel that life is a little chaotic and that you are stretched thin, take a moment to list all of the things that you are doing. Also make a note of how much time you spend with each activity and also the reasons why you are doing them. You will be surprised with what you will list down. As I created my list I was surprised with what I spent my time doing and the reasons why I did them. I realized I spent way too much time surfing the internet on websites like facebook and that some of the activities that I was involved were out of obligation not because I wanted to be a part of them. By creating this list you will notice what is on your plate and then you will be able to create more balance in your life.

STOP PILING MORE ON YOUR PLATE

Imagine right now that it's Thanksgiving. You are starving and cannot wait for the feast to begin. Finally the dinner starts and you grab your first plate. You get your hands on a piece of turkey, some corn bread, stuffing and a big scoop of creamy mash potatoes. Within a couple minutes you devour the food on your plate and you are on to your second plate. Eventually you reach a point where you no longer feel hungry and you are so full that it hurts. Every breath that you take makes you wince in pain. You begin to feel tired from the turkey and you want to take a nap but as you move yourself into position to do so, someone yells out, "pumpkin pie anyone?" Even though you are way too full, you justify to yourself, 'it's only one piece' so you eat it. Again you add more food to your plate. As

32

you slowly consume the pumpkin pie you regret your decision. After you finish the pie you feel worse than you did before! Have you ever had an experience like this where you ate too much?

This analogy is typical of what many people do in life. Their plates are full with activities and responsibilities ranging from taking on extra assignments at work, volunteering extra time for good causes or staying for a couple of extra hours a day to finish a project, and they keep piling more things on their plates which creates more stress, frustration and unhappiness.

It is common for some high school and college students do everything above and beyond the usual load. One of my best friends in colleges was like that. He was the team captain for the club soccer team, he was a vice president for the inter-fraternal council, worship leader for the local young adult ministries, worked at two different jobs on campus and on top of that he was a science major!!! Talk about having a full plate. You can only imagine what he was going through. As one of his best friends, I could see the stress and frustration that he was experiencing. He felt helpless because he was involved in so many things. This feeling only changed when it became too much for him that he had to withdraw into himself from some of his leadership positions. Immediately when he removed some of the "helpings" on his plate you could see the change in his face and attitude. The stress disappeared from his face and his overall attitude changed for the better. I actually wanted to be around him then.

If you are guilty of piling too much on your plate like my good friend (myself included) it is ok. It's important to be able to recognize that you have too much going on and you must make a decision to stop adding more to your plate if you are feeling overwhelmed.

SIMPLIFYING YOUR LIFE

We have all heard about the importance of being in balance in every area of our lives, our health, relationships, work and time with ourselves. That is easier said than done! Don't you wish that someone would actually teach you how to do it?

I once asked one of my mentors what her secret was to staying in balance and she shared with me a simple but profound idea. She told me, "Hoan, just simplify your life. Focus only on a couple of important things." As a young and ambitious person this was difficult for me to grasp. I wanted to do everything but what I began to realize is that sometimes less is more. When you focus on doing a couple of things you will get more done then trying to do a million things at once.

The important point is to de-clutter your life. Get rid of the things that you don't enjoy, may not be as important or that is just wasting your time.

PLANNING YOUR DAY

Benjamin Franklin said, "Failing to plan is planning to fail." If you talk with anybody, no one plans to fail, what they fail to do is plan. So to set yourself up to win always plan your day on paper the night before. There are two important things that I just mentioned. 1) The night before and 2) Planning on paper. By planning your day the night before you save a lot of precious time the following day. The second part, planning on paper is important because you are more likely to finish what you need to get done because you can see it. There is a saying, "a dull pencil is better than a sharp mind." Trust me, when you try to memorize everything you will forget something that is important. By planning everything on paper you will not forget the important things that you want to get done for that specific day.

While planning people usually write down a list of everything they have to do and by the end of the day they are frustrated because they did not finish their entire list. To prevent this from happening, have a set of questions and a routine when planning so your results are positive and measurable. Here is an example of mine:

- What are the two most important outcomes that I can accomplish today?
- What are two actions that I can do today that will help me move closer toward my goals?
- What are some of the things that I needed to get done today that I didn't get to?
- Who do I need to speak with tomorrow?

CAN YOU SCHEDULE ME IN?

If you don't have one already, purchase a day planner. It will be one of the best investments that you make. If you want something important to get done then you must schedule it. Write it down in your calendar at a specific time where you will focus solely on finishing that specific activity. A perfect example of this is classes in school. You have classes at certain times of the day on specific days. You schedule your classes in your day planner and you go. Make sure when blocking out time to eliminate all the distractions. (i.e. cell phone, internet)

TURNING KNOWLEDGE INTO ACTION

1. What is currently on your plate? Make a list of activities and things that currently occupy your time and how much each activity takes up on a daily basis (I.e. Work, School)

_____

_____

_____

2. Is your plate overflowing? What can you do today to simply your life? Is it saying no more often when people ask for a favor? Watching less TV?

_____

_____

_____

3. What are some questions that you can have that will help you plan each day?

_____

_____

_____

4. What are some things that you need to block out in your schedule that you want to get done?

_____

_____

_____

TAKE-AWAYS

- We all only have 24 hours in a day. Having balance is about make better choices with what we do with our time
- What are you spending your time doing? By listing down everything that you spend your time doing and the reasons why you do them, you then will be able to create more balance in your life.

- Don't pile more responsibilities on your plate if it is already overfilled
- Don't overcomplicate life. Simplify your life by focusing on a couple of important things rather than many unimportant things.
- Plan every day on paper the night before.
- Whenever you want to finish a task, make a point to schedule it into your calendar and remove all possible distractions

CHAPTER 4:

RELATIONSHIPS - KEEPING OLD FRIENDS, MEETING NEW FRIENDS, AND GETTING ALONG WITH OTHERS

"The glory of friendship is not the outstretched hand, nor the kindly smile, nor the joy of companionship; it is the spiritual inspiration that comes to one when he discovers that someone else believes in him and is willing to trust him."

~ *Ralph Waldo Emerson,* American Philosopher and Poet

One major difference you'll see when you graduate is the change in your social life. In college, everyone is in the same boat trying to figure out what to do after college, while still stressing over term papers and having conversations on dating. College is a collection of like-minded people going through the same experiences. As a result, it is easy to meet and relate with others. You go to class, sit next to a new person and you possibly become friends. When you feel like hanging out with your friends, you shoot them a quick text, find out what is happening later that night, and then you walk across campus to their apartment.

In the real world, adult life comes as a shock to many. In life after college, most of your friends live elsewhere and you more than likely will work with people who are older, may have kids and are at a different place in their lives. It may be more difficult to relate with them than with your classmates from college.

WHERE DID ALL OF MY FRIENDS GO?

After forging tight friendships for the last four or five years, the day after graduation, those bonds seem to sever as everyone goes their own way. Your roommate moves to another state for graduate school, and your best friend returns home to begin a career. Suddenly you realize all of your close friends whom you used to see everyday are now hundreds of miles away.

My best friends are now scattered all around the country. Two of them live in California and the other is living in Connecticut. I speak with them often because I believe in the importance of staying in touch with close friends, but I don't see them often. So with most of my friends not living nearby, I had to make new friends.

HIGH SCHOOL ALL OVER AGAIN

Take a moment and think back to your first days in high school. Can you remember when you were meeting all those new people? As you were meeting them, you were figuring out who you might connect with and who you might hangout with next. This is similar to life after college. Whether you go to graduate school or get a job, you are going to meet a lot of new people and make new friends. A challenge you might encounter is meeting other people your age. If I were to be honest with you, I would say that your new social life after school will be a lot different. In college, you are surrounded by people your age who are experiencing the same things you are. The real world is the opposite; however, you can still find other people your age to relate to; it is just going to take a little more effort on your end.

After I graduated, I went back home to Washington to work. As a professional speaker, unlike with many jobs that recent graduates get, I didn't go into an office to work; I worked out of my home. Most of my co-workers worked around the country from their home offices, so I worked mostly by myself. It was weird going from a college environment where I had my close friends living across the hall to working at my house with no one to talk to face to face. When I did see my colleagues, we had fun, but at times it was tough to relate to them on a personal level because they were ten years older than me and at a different stage of life. For a couple of months, I had a tough time. I was happy with my career, but I felt like I had no social life because everyone I would come in contact with on a day-to-day basis was older. Because of my situation, I made it a goal and intention that I would find other like-minded young people.

Here are a couple of tips for finding other young graduates you can connect with:

Hobbies and Interests

A great way to meet other people is through your interests. If you are into sports, join a local sports team. If you like to volunteer, find a non-profit you are passionate about helping.

University Alumni Chapters

This is a great place to connect with recent graduates. Most schools have alumni chapters located in every state.

Young Professional Groups

Are you an up-and-coming medical professional? Do you work in a particular industry? In every field, there is a national organization that brings together professionals within that industry.

It is important to find a great group of quality friends you can trust, relate to and rely on. Having good friends is important in order to succeed in the real world because the people you spend your time with have a huge affect on what you do and who you become.

Have you ever shared a dream or goal with a friend who said to you "Come on, be realistic" or "You can't do that because…" and then gave you a rational, level headed response that made you stop and come back to the realities of your life? The power of good friends is that they act as guiding forces that help us (hopefully) to make good rational decisions. Other people's comments can affect our beliefs, and our beliefs affect our attitude and what we do. We need others in our lives who are positive, help to build us up personally, and help us do what is right when making important decisions. We need to have the strength and the conviction to remove those so called "friends" who are not working toward similar goals and aspirations, do not support us, or who are holding us down.

In high school, I was a big time wrestler. During my junior year, I decided to commit myself to being one of the best wrestlers in my weight class in the state. At the time, I was struggling in my pre-calculus class. I had to make a decision on my priorities in life and what I was going to do. Deciding to focus on wrestling and my academics, I began spending less time hanging out on weeknights and weekends. When I made this decision, my friends at the time started to make fun of me and talk behind my back because I stopped hanging out with them. They said I was lame for studying and that I was a loser for not going to parties with them on the weekends. They got into drinking, partying and drugs while I focused on wrestling and school.

After graduating high school, I went down to California for school while all of them stayed in state. I haven't spoken to those friends since high school; I'm not sure what they are doing or where they are now; what I do know is that if I continued to hang out with them and had them in my circle of friends I wouldn't be where I am today. The friends I have now are the best because they are supportive of me and my dreams, and they inspire me to continue working hard toward my goals.

HAVING MENTORS IN YOUR LIFE

When they graduate, many students jump into life without a clear idea of where they are going or how they will proceed with their life now that they are finished with school. Having an experienced mentor or someone to guide you can save you a lot of time and prevent you from making costly mistakes. You can compare a mentor to having a coach in a sport. Athletes can perform well, but with a coach, they can do better because a coach can see what the athlete can't. Coaches usually have experience and have been successful in the sport themselves. Who I am today and what I have achieved I credit to having great mentors in my life to guide me.

Senior year is the year where you begin to think to yourself, "What am I going to do after college?" As I was in the process of interviewing for the Anthony Robbins Companies, I bumped into one of my good friends. He told me, "Hoan, you are going to love me! I just came back from spring break and have I got some news for you. I know you like Tony Robbins, and I wanted to let you know that my friend's father, Mike Hutchison, helped Tony Robbins at the beginning stages of his career." After Brendon said that, I thought, "You got to be kidding me!" Eventually, I got the opportunity to speak to Mike, and he shared with me his stories of working with the Robbins Company as well as some insights for the interview. We really connected, and I asked him whether he would mind if we stayed in touch.

After I landed a position with the company, Mike would call me occasionally to check in and see how I was doing. During our conversations, I would share with him my successes and also my challenges and struggles. He would always lend an ear to listen and share with me sound advice from a person who has lived and experienced a lot more of life than I have. We still talk on an ongoing basis.

A lot of young people know the importance of having mentors, but many wonder how you go about getting one. Here are my suggestions:

- Ask yourself, "Who do I look up to and respect in my life?" This can be a family member, friend, professor or older friend.

- After you determine the people you look up to, take them out to lunch so you can get to know them.
- After lunch, thank them and ask whether they would mind if you stayed in touch with them whenever you have any questions or need advice.

THAT PERSON IS DIFFERENT. I DON'T LIKE THEM

Have you ever been on a sports team or group project where there was that one person you did not get along with or couldn't stand? I am here to tell you there will be many of these people you will come in contact with professionally and personally after school.

In the real world, you will meet many new people from different backgrounds, values and beliefs. There will be many you can relate to and that you won't connect with. A place where you will be sure to experience this is at work.

In my first job after college, my boss and I would often find ourselves on two different ends of the spectrum. Often we would disagree or argue on many topics. This was frustrating to me because I am a really easy going guy. If you find yourself in a similar situation, here are two tips:

1. *Seek first to understand*

Find out where the other person is coming from. With my situation with my boss, we were often in disagreement because we each focused on our own objective and what we needed to get done without considering the other person. Try putting yourself in the other person's shoes and see situations from his or her perspective.

2. *Do your best*

What I realized is that relationships are a two way street. Make an effort to try to make things work; if the other person doesn't reciprocate, then at least you can say that you tried.

In using these two tips, my boss and I were able to gain a better understanding of one another. At times we still argued, but overall, we were better able to get along.

BUILDING A COMMUNITY OF FRIENDS

I feel fortunate that I get to meet interesting people from all over the world on a regular basis. I have friends all over the United States, in Europe, Asia and Australia. My friends are in different lines of work and come from different walks of life.

What I want to encourage you to do is to make lots of friends with all kinds of people because it will benefit you personally and professionally. I have gotten jobs and business through my network of friends as well as places to stay when I travel.

In school, they always talk about the importance of networking, but they never really teach you how to do it. As a student I would always think, "What do I have to offer people? I'm just a seventeen year old kid." What I want you to do is instead of thinking of meeting new people as networking, view it as making new friends. It helps make it less intimidating. Treat people you meet like an ordinary friend. Get to know them, stay in contact with them, and find out how you can help one another.

When I was younger, I was not as outgoing as I am today. I met a mentor in college who explained to me the importance of making friends with a community of people because you will have more fun and you never know how you can help one another in the future. Throughout my life, I have been fortunate to meet a lot of very successful people. When I decided to have a book launch party for this book, many of these people wanted to help me. I was featured in three well-known newspapers; we were also able to get food and drinks donated at our event for no charge.

WE SHOULD HANGOUT! I WILL CALL YOU LATER

Do you have a friend or know of someone who always says, "We should hang out! I will call you later" and then they never call?

Another important lesson I have learned about relationships is the importance of staying in touch. Everything that is achieved in life is through relationships, whether it's getting a job, finding a new home, getting advice through tough times, it's people who will help you with all of it. The major problem is that people are very bad at staying in touch. I don't know why because there are so many easy ways to stay in touch from email to Facebook. Make an effort to stay in touch with people that you meet; especially the people that you would like to continue and develop a friendship with.

TURNING KNOWLEDGE INTO ACTION

1. A good place to begin meeting interesting people is through your hobbies and interests. What do you enjoy doing? Do you like playing basketball, or are you looking for a church or organization to be a part of? List some of your favorite activities in the space below:

_____

_____

_____

2. Take a moment and ask yourself, are the people you 'hang out' with pulling you forward (i.e. supporting you in your goals) or holding you back (i.e. criticizing you for your goals)? If the latter, do you need to make a change in friends?

_____

_____

_____

3. Whom do you admire or look up to that you could take to lunch? When will you reach out to them?

_____

_____

_____

TAKE-AWAYS

- Relationships (friendships and intimate) that you have in the real world are very different than in school.
- Your choice of friends is crucial. They can make a positive or negative impact on you.
- Have mentors in your life to guide you. This will help you through the tough times.
- When meeting people you don't click or get along with, seek to understand and see situations from their perspectives. Try your best to connect with them; if they don't reciprocate, it's okay; at least you tried.
- Stay in touch; stay connected.

CHAPTER 5:

STRESS - OMG! ARE YOU KIDDING ME?

"In times of great stress or adversity, it's always best to keep busy,
to plow your anger and your energy into something positive."

~ Lee Iacocca, American Businessman

Going through life it is inevitable that we will experience stress, frustration, and adversity. Now more than ever I believe that there is more pressure on young people. We are expected to find a job, figure out if we are making the right decisions as well as deal with the pressures of day to day life. I flipped through thick textbooks looking for ways to manage the stresses from life. Unfortunately none of them provided answers on how to deal with the roller coaster of emotions that one goes through during this time.

THE PRESSURESOF BEING YOUNG

What do you want to do with your life? Where are you going to work? Where are you going to live? These are only a handful of the questions that you are probably bombarded with right now and let me tell you that this won't stop after graduation.

I am not going to lie, after leaving school there is a lot more to think about then you have ever been faced with in your life. Doubts begin to creep in; questions arise when making important decisions. Life may not be exactly what you expected. Working might not be what you imagined. You might find you comparing yourself with others. You might be feeling alone because friends are not near you. There is a lot to think about when entering adulthood.

WHY DOES THIS ALWAYS HAPPEN TO ME?

Have you ever had days where everything seems to go wrong? You wake up and stub your toe on your bed frame; you leave your apartment and realize that you forgot your cell phone?

You may experience times in your life where you feel that everything is stacked against you and when something could possibly go wrong that it does. Rather than falling into the trap that life is against you and that you are unlucky, embrace this quote by Mother Theresa:

"In life there are no problems, only gifts."

A couple of months after graduating and beginning my career I received devastating news about someone very close to me. A person that I was very close with was going through a gambling addiction. This addiction did not only affect me but also my family. It was hard for me to see this person because I tried everything that I could to help but nothing worked. Here I was the guy who helped and coached other people through their life challenges and I couldn't even help one of my close friends. Because this was so close to home, I constantly would think about this situation and in doing so it also affected my work life. I was distracted and found my results at work to be lower than normal. Eventually my boss called me to ask me about the decline in my performance. He mentioned to me that if this continued and my results did not improve that I would no longer be working with the company. After hearing this I thought to myself, "why me?" As

48

if things weren't worse enough I was about to be fired!

This was the first major challenge that I faced in my life after college. This was a very trying difficult time. Fortunately a mentor said to me, "Many things happen in life that we can't describe. That's a part of life. Use this to develop your character. "

After speaking with my mentor, I sat down, focused and asked myself, "What good can I take away from this? What can I learn from this experience?" I came up with ideas like how this experience would strengthen my faith and also that this experience will be a story that can inspire others in similar situations. Because of the support and encouragement of those close to me, as well as my decision to focus on the learning lessons that I could take away from the situation, I was able to overcome this challenge in my life.

I am a big believer that everything in life happens for a reason, even if it may be an unpleasant experience or something that you didn't want to happen. It is in those moments where the gift is the lesson you take away, what you learn and who you become.

DO YOU CONTROL EVENTS OR DO THEY CONTROL YOU?

In life, when something bad or unfortunate happens, many people allow the event to control and affect them. A great example is the economy; with all of the negative news floating around about the job market it's easy to feel stressed out. Given you cannot control what happens with the economy, the part that you can control is what it means to you and what you do about it.

I allowed my concern for my friend's gambling addiction to control my emotions and me. The fact that I was not able to support him was painful for me. This then affected my work life which led me to almost being fired. What helped me to overcome this stressful and challenging situation was when I took control of this event by focusing on how this experience would help me to become a better person to help others in similar situations. By changing my perspective on the situation I was able to overcome this difficult situation.

The next time that you find yourself in a difficult situation and that everything seems to be going against you, consider these two points as they will help put you in control of an event rather than the event controlling you.

1. Acknowledge the fact that the only thing that you can control is what something means to you and how you react to it

2. Ask yourself questions that will help you to relieve stress and to refocus into a state of mind where you are resourceful and able to take action to handle your situation. Some examples are

- What can I take away from this situation?

- How can I use this experience to help others?

BREATHE IN, BREATHE OUT

Whenever you find yourself stressed or frustrated, here are three simple and practical things that you can do to reduce or eliminate these feelings.

1. *Move around*

Usually when stressed, frustrated or upset if you pay attention a person will have a certain posture about them. Their face may be scrunched up, they may have shallow breathing. Change your emotional state by moving your body. Go for a walk or go exercise. You will notice that you will always feel better afterward.

2. *Take a break away from what is frustrating you*

Read a book or one of my favorite things to do is to listen to music. This will help you clear your mind so that you can go back with a fresh perspective.

3. *Express yourself*

One of the best things that you can do when you are frustrated, or feeling angry is to find a way to get that stress out of your system. Whether it is through talking to a friend or writing in a journal you must get it out of your system. Too many people bottle things up inside. Doing this will make you feel worse in the long term and all of a sudden like a soda can that has been shaken up so much, the person eventually explodes.

STOP BEATING YOURSELF UP

If you ever got into a fist fight, would you begin hitting yourself? We may not beat ourselves up physically but we often beat up ourselves emotionally whether it's getting angry at ourselves for making a mistake or not doing something right. Realize that you will make mistakes; it's a natural part of life. Don't beat yourself up but learn from those mistakes and next time make smarter decisions.

Wayne Dyer, author and lecturer says that all of us walk around with a bag of guilt behind us. Whenever we make a mistake we turn around and open up this bag to remind ourselves. Realize that you can't change the past, you can only learn from your mistakes. So stop beating yourself up because it does not do you any good.

TURNING KNOWLEDGE INTO ACTION

1. Can you remember a challenging time where you felt that everything that could go wrong happened? How did you overcome that situation? What was the gift or lesson that you took away? How has this gift helped you today or how can it help you today as you run into more life challenges?

_____

_____

_____

2. Think about a situation that you are experiencing right now that is causing you stress and frustration. What questions can you ask yourself that can help you change your perspective so that you can control the event rather than having it control you?

_____

_____

_____

3. Is there any mistakes that you have made in your life that you regret and beat yourself up over? Take a moment and write them below. After you list them, acknowledge that you made these mistakes. Realize that you cannot go back and change them and make a decision to move forward.

_____

_____

_____

TAKE-AWAYS

- There are a lot of pressure and stresses of being a young person
- When you find yourself in stressful or challenging situations don't see it as that life is stacked against you. View the situation as a gift where you will learn something new rather than a problem.
- Don't let events of life control you. Remember that you control what a situation means to you and how you react to it. To help you focus, ask yourself questions like "what can I take away from this experience."
- When you feel stressed or frustrated, get some exercise, and take a break from what is frustrating you or talk to a friend.
- Don't beat yourself up anymore. Realize that making mistakes is ok.

CHAPTER 6:

FEAR - STEPPING OUTSIDE OF YOUR COMFORT ZONE

"All our dreams can come true if we have the courage to pursue them."

~ Walt Disney, Founder of Disney Land and Disney World

During your time in school, I imagine you have been stretched outside of your comfort zone many times, from making new groups of friends to making tough decisions. In the real world, you can expect the same. You will face difficult challenges and new experiences like not getting along with co-workers, questioning whether you made the right career choice, and second guessing decisions you make. This chapter is dedicated to supporting you in dealing with your fears and concerns.

WHAT IF...

What if I follow my dreams and don't reach them? What if I try to live on my own and can't make it? What if I can't handle the stresses and responsibilities of being an adult? It's easy for our minds to wander and think about the possibility of how situations can turn out. Fear is natural. Being scared is a sign that whatever you may be scared about is important. Many people don't like feeling fearful because it's uncomfortable. Rather than trying to avoid or dread this feeling, embrace it. Instead of thinking of it as a bad or negative feeling, try to see it as a positive feeling because when you're scared, it means you are doing something outside of your comfort zone.

ARE YOU AFRAID? AWESOME! THAT MEANS YOU ARE GROWING

A year ago, we had company training for all of our speakers and trainers. During our training, we had a former colleague who came back to share her story about how she became successful for the company. During her talk, she asked us what was important in our lives, what we wanted to achieve, and what impact we wanted to have. After we took a minute to think about our answers to her questions, she made this very profound statement.

"Everything that you want is right outside of your comfort zone."
~ Nuirka, Speaker and Life Coach

Whether it's being physically fit, positioning yourself to be financially well off, or being in your ideal relationship, to achieve these goals you will have to do things that are outside your comfort zone.

I remember in my first year of college, I lived in a suite with three students who were theatre majors. These guys were talented—acting, singing, dancing, you name it. I always wanted to learn how to sing, but I never took the time to learn because I was scared by the thought of singing in public. I was already scared enough to sing when my friends were around because I was horrible at it. After two years of complaining how I wish I knew how to sing, my friends finally convinced me to build up the courage to take an introductory voice class.

It was the first day of class, and as in any class, our professor asked us to introduce ourselves and to share any background we had in singing. As we went around the room, a student raised her hand, shared her name, and said she came from a family of musicians

54

and had been singing since she was ten. Next a tall, skinny guy introduced himself and said that he had been singing his entire life, and that he was part of the school's praise and worship team. I thought to myself, "What on earth? I thought this was an introductory voice lesson class?" When it came my turn to introduce myself, I said, "I have been singing my entire life, mostly in the shower and in the car." Everyone started to laugh. My initial thought was, "Oh brother, this is going to be one long semester." After the introductions, we jumped right into the mechanics of singing. We practiced exercises that strengthened our diaphragms and our singing voices. At the end of the class, the professor gave us a song sheet to memorize for the following class when we would have to come up and sing it in front of the class.

My jaw dropped. As I walked out of class, I thought to myself, "WHAT HAVE I GOTTEN MYSELF INTO?" Over the next week, I rehearsed repeatedly to make sure I wouldn't mess up. Before I knew it, one week had passed, and it was time to go back to the class. I was scared out of my mind. The experienced students went first, and they had no problem. I could feel my stomach tighten as it came closer to my turn. Then all of a sudden, it was time. I slowly walked in front of the classroom, and before anything came out of my mouth, I thought to myself, people say that the number one fear above death is public speaking. NO WAY! Singing in public is worse than that. The professor played the song and I began to sing. It was HORRRIBLE. I could feel and hear the trebling in my voice. I didn't look anyone in the eye because I was afraid I would forget my words or that someone would laugh at me. Those thirty seconds were the longest thirty seconds of my entire life. After I sang, I was so relieved. Week after week, we would sing in front of the class. Each time I was scared, but the more I sang in public, the better and more confident I became. Toward the end of the semester, when I sang my final song, I found the fear subsiding and felt more comfortable singing in front of others. At the end of the class, I felt even more confident in myself and decided to enroll in the next level course in voice lessons.

Learning how to sing was one of the skills I always wanted to acquire. The only way I was going to learn how to sing was to be willing to step outside of my comfort zone and do something I feared. Because I took voice lessons, not only did I benefit from learning how to sing, but I also took away valuable lessons and insights, and I became more confident in my public speaking and more comfortable with myself as a person.

GETTING RID OF THE JITTERS

Do you ever find yourself feeling nervous or scared regardless of how much preparation you do? There will be many times when you will feel doubt and moments when you second guess yourself. Whether it is during a job interview or making the decision to change careers, you will ALWAYS get the jitters or second guess yourself. The two biggest things that have helped me to calms my nerves is having the right focus and having faith.

1. Focus

When I began my career as a speaker with Tony Robbins, I often found myself getting nervous before every one of my presentations. I would always worry about what I was going to say and how I was going to say it. One of the senior speakers gave me a suggestion that helped me to feel less nervous. He said that if you ever feel fearful, that means you are focusing too much on yourself. You think about what if I mess up, what if other people will say something about me. Instead of asking yourself, "What do I need to say, how should I say it, and what will the audience think about me?" ask yourself, "What value can I provide? What do I appreciate most about these people?" By asking these different questions, you will find that the fear will disappear.

2. Faith

If you have done all you can to prepare yourself, then just believe that everything will be okay. If you over worry, it won't do you any good. There is no benefit in over worrying. Prepare yourself to the best of your ability, and after you do that, just have faith.

READY...FIRE...AIM

There are many people who get ready, they aim...and never fire because they are fearful that every possible bad thing that could happen will happen. Many times, instead of getting ready, aiming and then firing, there are times when we just need to get ready, fire and re-aim afterwards.

Now I am not saying to not think things through and to act on hunches. You should always make decisions with thoughts behind them. There comes a point sometimes though where you just over think a situation. You know when you are doing this. When you find yourself over thinking, that's when you need to follow Nike's slogan "JUST DO IT!" The best way to reduce your fear or to gain more confidence is just to go and do what you find most fearful. What you fear most is probably what you NEED to do the most. Stop thinking and start doing.

During my early years in college, I interned and worked for a motivational speaker by the name of Art Mortell. My job was to set speaking engagements for Art through telemarketing. This was my first experience working in sales. My days would consist of making telephone calls to Vice Presidents of Sales and sales managers at companies across the U.S. I can remember my very first call. This is how it went: Hi, my name is Hoan Do with Dynamics of Human Potential; I represent a motivational speaker by the name of Art Mortell. – Sorry. Not interested. Click. I was devastated.

This was my first experience of having a person hang up on me. After my first day, this became a regular thing. I would call. People would say not interested, and they would hang up on me. Occasionally I would have people nicely say, "We will call you back later," which they never did. This didn't soften the blow; it was not fun being rejected day in and day out. This was not glamorous at all. After getting rejected so many times, I felt the phone become heavier. Many times I would fumble my words and get nervous. After making over a hundred phone calls, slowly, as I made more calls and spoke to more executives and managers, I became better at what I did. I realized that by making more calls, I felt more comfortable and confident. Building courage was like building muscle. The more time you exercise your muscles, the stronger they get. The same is true with building your courage to act when you're scared or fearful.

FEAR OF REGRET

Many times people stop pursuing their goals and dreams because of the fear of failure or rejection. A fear I think should be greater is the fear of regret. I think what is worse than the feeling of failing short of a goal is to look back and ask yourself "What if...?" or "Could I have...?"

As I worked for Tony Robbins, I spent a large portion of my time with people who were older than I was, consulting and coaching them in life. In our conversations, one of the most common regrets that they shared was foregoing their dreams and passions because they believed those dreams were not realistic or practical. Their dreams ranged from pursuing a career they were interested in to going on a date with a person they found attractive. Many of these people carry regret with them still today, wondering how their lives would have been different had they made different decisions.

Are there any situations you have been debating about in your life because of the potential fear of failure? If so, consider this quote by Theodore Roosevelt, our 26th President:

> *"Far better is it to dare mighty things, to win glorious triumphs,*
> *even though checkered by failure...than to rank with those*

poor spirits who neither enjoy nor suffer much, because they

live in a gray twilight that knows not victory nor defeat."

TURNING KNOWLEDGE INTO ACTION

1. What is something you fear that you know you need to do because if you did it, it would have a positive impact on your life?

_____

_____

_____

2. What is the absolute worst thing that could happen if you did what you feared most?

_____

_____

_____

3. What would be the best thing that could happen by doing something you want but fear to do?

_____

_____

_____

4. By putting off what you know you need, what is it costing you? Emotionally, physically, financially and/or spiritually?

_____

_____

_____

TAKE-AWAYS

- Fear is natural. Rather than viewing it as a negative emotion, see it as something positive because it means you are growing by doing something you are not used to doing.

- Everything you want is outside of your comfort zone.

- To calm your nerves and to reduce your fear, stop focusing on yourself and have faith that everything will be okay.

- Take your time and think things through, but don't OVER THINK. When you find yourself over thinking, remember Nike's slogan, "Just do it!" By doing what you fear, you will exercise and strengthen your courage muscle.

- Don't live in regret. The greatest fear should not be failure or rejection; it should be a fear of regret. Don't be the person who says to him or herself, "I wish I would have" or "What if?"

CHAPTER 7:

CAREER - HOW TO LAND ANY JOB YOU WANT

"The decisions you make about your work life is especially important,
since most people spend most of their waking lives working than
doing anything else. Your choices will affect, not only yourself
and those closest to you, but in some way the whole world."

~ Laurence G. Boldt, Author

It's a competitive world out there. An important decision that we have to make as we move from student life to real life is selecting a career. Poll any group of college seniors and ask them what their greatest concern is after they graduate and more than likely they will all say, "Finding a job." You knew the day would eventually come when you would enter the work force and become an adult. I'm here to tell you that it's not as bad as you might think. I dedicated this entire chapter to showing you step-by-step what you can do to go from being confused and unemployed to being confident and landing any position you want.

IF YOU COULD DO ANYTHING, WHAT WOULD YOU WANT TO DO?

You have probably been asked this by everybody. You might be thinking, "Oh my gosh, I hear that all of the time; I just don't know." If you are thinking this, I am here to let you know it is okay. There are many people who are in their forties and fifties who still don't know what they would like to do.

Many students graduate and end up working at a place they don't like because they never got clear about what wanted in a career. Often students scramble during the last semester and settle for any job they can get, or they pursue a career route for the wrong reasons because it can make them a lot of money or because someone told them they should do it. This is a big mistake. Your career will be a big part of your life. You will spend many hours of your life working. So why not do something you enjoy? Now I want to make it clear that there is nothing wrong with choosing a job because you can make a good living. I believe you can do something you enjoy and make a good living at it as well. I like what Confucius had to say about work:

"If you find a job you love, you will never work a day in your life."

So the first thing you need to consider when thinking about what you are going to do after school is to identify what it is you want in a job after school. What it is that you enjoy doing?

THE SEARCH BEGINS

Once you have listed your passions, what you enjoy doing, and what you are looking for in a job, the next question is "Where can I do what I enjoy and be paid for it?" There are many resources to help you find a career that fits your match. Below are a couple of resources of where you can look to find potential places to work:

- Career Center

  I think that the career center is one of the most under utilized resources in school. The career center has counselors who are there to help you find a job after you graduate, along with useful information for writing a resume, cover letters etc.

- Mentors, Professors, Parents

  Let them know what your plans are and what you are looking for in a job. They may know of another person who is looking for someone just like you. During my junior year, I was interested in real estate investing, and I told one of my mentors at home, and he told me that his son owned a couple of companies that did real estate investing. That summer I worked as an intern for his son.

- Internet

  There are many websites out there that will help you to find companies that are hiring like monster.com.

One of the best places to look for a job is at the companies where you buy the services or gadgets. Let's pretend you love Apple Computers (sorry pc users); your place is decked out with an iPod, iBook—you name it, you've got it. You really enjoy graphic designs so why not find out if Macintosh has any open positions doing what you would enjoy?

I eventually found the first company that I worked for straight out of college because I liked their products and used their services.

BECOMING THE CANDIDATE EMPLOYERS ARE LOOKING FOR

Once you identify some companies where you would like to work, you have to work on making yourself the best candidate possible. The question that you have to think about is: what will you bring to the table that will make employers want you?

After meeting and interviewing many human resources experts, here are three important factors that will make you stand out when interviewing:

1. *Do you have experience?*

By experience, I don't mean classroom experience; I mean real life experience. In school, your GPA measures whether you are qualified. In life, it is experience. Unless you are going to graduate school, your GPA isn't weighed heavily upon in deciding to hire a person for a position. Employers want to know whether you can get the job done. Get real life work experience in the field or line of work that interests you. When I knew that I wanted to work for the Anthony Robbins Companies as a speaker, I interned with local speakers, and I spoke to high schools, colleges and companies so I could prove to the company that I could handle the responsibilities of that job.

2. *Good Attitude*

This sounds so simple, yet it is so important. Companies are looking for positive people to be a part of their teams because a person with a bad attitude will negatively impact the entire company.

3. *Coachable*

Are you willing to learn and try new things? Many companies look for people whom they can mold and mentor. They want someone who can listen and take feedback.

GETTING YOUR FOOT IN THE DOOR

After you decide on what you want to do and what companies you might like to work for, the next step is getting an interview. Most college students and recent graduates spend large amounts of time making their resumes look perfect. They then usually go to the company website and submit a resume online and hope they get a call back. The truth is that the chances of getting a call back using this method is low because companies get so many applications that it's hard for them even to keep count. If you are trying to get interviews, make a follow up call to the company to check on the status of your resume/application. Even if you do this, you may still not get an interview.

The fastest and easiest way to get an interview is by having someone refer you or pass your name to the right person. It is a lot easier to get an interview from a person referring you than blindly submitting an application because the referral will come from someone the interviewer trusts. Think about if you saw a movie preview; if it didn't really excite you, would you go watch it? Probably not. What if twenty of your friends told you that you had to watch the movie? Because of their endorsement or feedback, would you re-consider watching it?

Don't get me wrong now; having a good resume and cover letter is important. I'm just saying that it won't guarantee you an interview. When I applied for a position to work with the Anthony Robbins Companies, a personal development company out of California, I sent in the most beautifully written and articulate resume and cover letter in the world. I even had about five to seven resume experts and professionals look over it. To my surprise, I received no response from the Robbins organization. After a week, I didn't even get a lousy email from the company. Fortunately after attending a seminar that the Anthony Robbins Companies had put together, I met a couple of people who worked there and stayed in touch with them. One of them said that he would pass my information to the right person for me. The same day that he sent in my resume and cover letter, I received a call from human resources for an interview.

This is the perfect example of the cliché saying, "It's not what you know, but who you know." You might be thinking, "I don't know anybody!" You might be surprised. Are you a part of a fraternity or sorority? Do your friend's parents' work at a place where you may be interested in working? Did you recently meet a friend through Facebook who has a friend who has a connection to the place where you want to apply? Through websites like Facebook and Linked In, you never know how people are connected to one another. Look through the network of people you know and see whether any of them have a connection that can help you to get an interview at the company where you would like to work.

Regardless of whether you get referred or send in your resume and application through the website, make sure you stay in touch with the companies where you applied for a position. If you don't hear back, give them a courtesy call or email. The biggest mistake students make is that they don't follow up. Follow up until they tell you that you didn't get an interview.

ACING THE INTERVIEW

Once you land an interview, you must get yourself ready to knock the interviewer's socks off. There is a saying that "prior preparation prevents poor performance." Prior preparation will be the deciding factor if you get hired because companies are looking for a great candidate who will represent them at the highest level.

Here are three tips to help you to prepare for and ace your interview:

1. *Do your research*

Get to know the company where you are applying. Find out important information about the company. It is not important to know how many employees they have and when their shareholders' meetings are held. You want to know what they do? What services do they provide? What is their company goal? These are some of the things to look for when you do your research on a company. Also a bonus would be to find out who will be interviewing you and learning about that person or people through the company website.

2. *Practice what you will say in an interview*

Too many people go in and try to "wing" the job interview. This is the biggest mistake a person can make. Why would you want to take a chance and wing it with an opportunity to land your dream job?

Look at the preparation it takes to be a specialty athlete like a football field goal kicker. In A field goal kicker's responsibilities include kicking the extra point and field goals. He is on the field for maybe five or so minutes total throughout a game. Not much at all, but guess how much time he puts into practicing for those few minutes? Kickers practice as much time or more as every other player on the field. Their job depends on it!

It is the same with the job interview. The more you practice, the better you will get. Find out the type of questions that might be asked at your interview and rehearse some prompted answers. For example a common question employers ask is, "What is your greatest weakness?" Wouldn't it make it a lot easier thinking up an answer well in advance and knowing what to say before the actual interview? Trying to think of the perfect answer on the spot is difficult.

Check your college's career center for support; find out the most commonly asked interview questions and sign up for mock interviews if possible. Practice for these questions. Go online or to your career center and find commonly asked questions and have set answers for them. The best thing you can do is actually practice in simulated interviews to get yourself more comfortable for the real thing.

Prior to my interview with the Anthony Robbins Companies, I applied at other companies and used those interviews as practice interviews to prepare me for the big one.

3. *Be Confident and Believe You Will Get the Job*

In the interview, you are selling the idea that you are the best candidate for them. After I got my foot in the door with the Anthony Robbins Companies, I had to go through four different interviews: two with a recruiter, one with the Vice President of Sales, and one group interview with the current speakers on the team. From the get go, I was tested and questioned in many ways. A recurring topic was that I was very young and lacked experience compared too many other candidates. I did not let this get to me because even though they thought I had little experience, I believed I had plenty of experience. I had interned with one of the top sales and motivational speakers of all time, I had already created my own real estate investment company, and I spoke regularly in front of audiences ranging from high school students to managers and owners of corporate businesses by the age of twenty-one. They believed that I had little experience? I proved through my confidence that I did have experience. And any that I lacked would come through my hunger and commitment to learn.

The Vice President of Sales was impressed with my confidence and assertiveness, so he told me that they wanted to give me a chance. They flew me down to San Diego for a four day training / interview. During this boot camp, I was among interviewee's from across the United States and Canada. Most of the applicants were at least five to ten years my senior. Even though I was the young "kid" there, I remained confident. A large portion of the interview was memorizing and rehearsing a thirty-page presentation to be delivered in front of the group. This alone was intimidating because throughout my speaking experience, I never had to remember anything this long. I felt as if I were an actor preparing and rehearsing for a show. I only had one week actually to memorize it.

I was the first one to be called up; I constantly reminded myself of how much I prepared for the position and how perfect I was for this position. I was certain this job was made for me. Because I exuded this confidence, not only did I believe that the job was right for me, but everyone else believed it as well and out of all the candidates, I was one of the five selected for the position.

THE FOLLOW UP

After you finish the interview, immediately follow up with a sincere thank you card. This is something that is so simple, but it makes a huge impression. There are many people who are taught to send out cards but rarely do, or they send out a generic "Thank you for your time; I look forward to hearing from you." The key to remember in writing these cards is don't just stick in a generic note. Personalize it. If the person who interviewed you had an interesting background or shared an interesting point, mention it in your card. You can say something along the lines of "It was great meeting you on Monday. I enjoyed learning more about your company and also about your previous experience with XYZ Company." By making the card personal, it will show employers that you were engaged and paid attention to what they said.

Many people don't send out thank you cards because they forget, it takes too much time or it cost too much. There is a really cool service I use called Send Out Cards. Its a very unique greeting card company that I have partnered with, where you can go online to choose a thank you card, type in your message and then click send and your done. Immediately afterward, a greeting card written in your handwriting is sent from the company on your behalf as if you sent it yourself, to the person you interviewed with for about a dollar. To learn more about it, feel free to shoot me an email.

I GOT THE JOB THAT I WANTED BUT I HATE IT

Some students are afraid they might get a job that they thought they would like and then find out it's not for them. I want you to know that this happens all the time, and it is okay. One of my good friends landed his dream job straight out of college, but by the end of his first year with the company, he said he hated it. Just know that if this happens to you, you can always work somewhere else. It is not the end of the world.

TURNING KNOWLEDGE INTO ACTION

1. If you could do anything, what would you want to do? Take a moment and make a list of things you enjoy doing or that interest you.

_____

_____

_____

2) Based on the list above, who is someone you can speak to (a career counselor, professor, mentor) today who could give you some guidance on companies that are hiring for positions doing what you enjoy? Or what Internet site can you go on today where you can search for companies where you would be interested in working?

_____

_____

_____

3. What can you do today to make you the best candidate possible? Could you apply to a related internship to get work experience? Can you work on being a better receiver of feedback?

_____

_____

_____

4. Make a list of companies you would like to work for and set aside today to check what positions they are hiring.

_____

_____

_____

TAKE-AWAYS

- When deciding what you plan to do after you graduate, choose a career path you are interested in or enjoy. The reason why many post-graduates don't enjoy what they do is because they settled for anything.

- Utilize your resources (career counselors, professors, family, and friends) to help you to find companies where you could work.

- Work on making yourself the best candidate possible by getting real world experience, having a good attitude and being coachable.

- Nice resumes and cover letters are great, but they won't guarantee that you will get an interview. Look through the network of people you know who may be able to get you an interview.

- To ace the interview:

  - Do your research—know the facts about the company.

  - Practice what you are going to say in an interview—rehearse commonly asked questions and have prearranged answers for the questions.

  - Believe that you will get the position—If you believe you are the right candidate, they will more likely believe you are as well.

- Follow up after the interview with a sincere thank you card. Make the card personal by bringing up specific points from your conversation.

CHAPTER 8:

FINANCES – SHOW ME THE MONEY!

"If you want to create wealth, it is imperative that you believe
that you are at the steering wheel of life; that you create every
moment of your life, especially your financial life."
~ T. Harv Eker, Best Selling Author and Financial Speaker

After college, many graduates find themselves surprised with new experiences like paying back school loans and debts, rent and more. Many think that after getting their first job, the living on a shoestring budget of a college student is over. Think again. Often graduates find themselves reverting back to their college days of pinching pennies.

In school, we were never taught how to succeed financially. We never learned the basics of money like keeping track of our money, how to invest or how to pay back school loans. Money and finances are a huge part of our lives and to ignore them would be silly, so I wanted to make sure I addressed this issue.

IS WANTING MONEY BAD?

After my family escaped the Vietnam War to begin a new life in America, we did not have a lot of resources. My family worked endless hours to make ends meet. Even though we did not come from a financially abundant family, my parents always found a way to provide for my brother and me. They found a way to buy me that special gift I always wanted, or they helped me to pay tuition to attend an expensive private college. Because of this experience, I made it a goal to become financially well off so I could take care of them in return.

Growing up, I always heard people say that money is the root of all evil. I saw it tear families apart, and I saw people steal just to have it. I was conflicted. It was not until I spoke with a good friend that my perspective about money changed. He helped me to understand that wanting money was not bad. It was the greed to do whatever it took to attain it even if it meant hurting other people that was bad. He helped me to understand that wanting to have a good life was not wrong. Being financially well off provides more opportunities to contribute.

As I mentioned in the first chapter of this book, our beliefs affect our attitude and our attitude impacts our decisions, which affect our results. Many people are never able to take care of this area of their lives because of the beliefs they have about money.

DOING WELL FINANCIALLY IS LEARNED

Growing up, I always thought people were either going to be well off financially or they weren't. I believed it was about luck until I ran into an old high school friend. At the time, I was eighteen, and he was twenty-one. When we sat down to lunch, I asked him what he was doing now. He told me he had been really busy running his three Subway restaurants and that he owned and managed six houses that he rented out. My jaw dropped when I heard this. I asked him, "What are you doing? Are you selling drugs?" He laughed and said, "No, what I did was I began reading books and learning from other people who were successful." Reconnecting with my friend inspired me to believe that
74

doing well financially was something that could be learned and worked at rather than something that was out of my control.

BUT IT'S TOO HARD

After meeting with my friend, he told me he wanted to share with me what he had learned. I appreciated his offer, but I told him that money and investing was difficult and confusing. He told me that just like everything else, it's always difficult at the beginning; it just takes time. He then recommended that I read two books. One was Think and Grow Rich by Napoleon Hill and the other was Rich Dad, Poor Dad by Robert Kiyosaki. Both of these books helped me to get a better grasp about money and the simple and important concepts I needed to understand.

What I realized is that for some people, money and finances are easy to follow. For me, it wasn't. But since I knew it would affect my life, I made a decision to persevere and learn.

INVESTING 101: HAVING YOUR MONEY WORK HARD FOR YOU

Investing can be confusing and scary to some because it was not touched on in any classes in school. Learning about the topic of investing is important because in your working life, you will work and be compensated for your time. If you stop working, you no longer make any money. But investing allows your money to work hard for you.

Here is a list of a few different ways you can invest:

- Stocks
- Mutual Funds
- Real Estate
- Businesses
- Bonds

- Certificates of Deposit (CD)

In seeing this list, I know it can be overwhelming. All this was to me at first. What I would suggest for you to do is to take some time and learn about the different options out there about investing. You will begin to understand what they are and what are the pros and cons of each investment. From there, you can choose the ones that are of most interest to you and that you would like to learn more about.

PAYING YOURSELF FIRST

An important concept I learned at an early age was the idea of paying yourself first. You have heard of this before; this concept is to encourage you to take 10% of what you make and to put it aside. I know you're probably thinking "With what money?" It's easy to pay your cell phone bill, credit card and rent and at the end of the month have nothing left over. This is the reason why many people don't get ahead financially in life. An easy way to insure that you save 10% is to have that amount taken from each of your checks and placed in a separate savings account.

After you have some money stored away, you can begin to invest your money.

WHERE DID ALL OF MY MONEY GO?

It's so easy to go to restaurant for lunch with friends and then go to a movie in the evening and then at the end of the month find out that you have no more money in your bank account. One of the biggest lessons I learned about finances was through this proverb:

"The art is not in making money, but in keeping it."

To begin to move in the right direction and get out of the broke college student days, you must first begin to keep track of where your money is coming from and where it is going too. Keep track of your purchases. One of the best ways is to print out a list of purchases you make for the month from your online bank account. I know this may sound simple, but to get ahead financially, you first have to spend less than you earn. Today with more and more people applying for credit cards, this can be difficult to do.

THE D WORD

Debt is not a fun topic to talk about. But the truth is that most college students leave college with debt in terms of school loans and credit cards. Figuring out how to deal with debt can be overwhelming. Here are two ideas that will help you to manage your debt:

1. *Don't over extend yourself.*

We live in a society where the national savings rate is negative. The reason why so many people today are struggling is because they over extend themselves. Make sure you keep your credit cards in check by watching what you purchase. Ask yourself if the item is a need or a want. (FYI - Getting the latest and coolest phone is not a need.)

2. *Pay all debts on time.*

If your school loans or credit cards have auto-debit payment, apply for it. What this does is that without you even having to think about it, monthly payments will be made to your loan or credit card. By doing this, it insures that you make your payments and some companies even give you an incentive so in the long run you pay a lot less.

THE BEST INVESTMENT IN THE WORLD

Would you like to learn about an investment that has no down side and only an upside? You are probably thinking that's impossible. The best investment that you can make is the investment of your time to educate yourself in the area of finance. I like the following quote by business philosopher and speaker Jim Rohn:

"Formal education will make you a living;

self-education will make you a fortune."

As a junior in college I was able to invest in real estate because of the years I put in learning and reading up on it. This did not happen overnight; it happened through two years of personal education through books, seminars and mentorship. Since school does not touch on this important topic, you have to make a decision to educate yourself. This choice will impact your financial well being.

TURNING KNOWLEDGE INTO ACTION

1. What are your beliefs around money? Are they positive or negative?

_____

_____

_____

2. What can you do today to increase your awareness and knowledge on the topic of money? (i.e. – Purchase a financial book, or visit with a financial planner)

_____

_____

_____

3. Do you currently keep track of where you spend your money? If you do, great. If not, what system can you put in place to help you keep track of your spending?

_____

_____

_____

TAKE-AWAYS

- Wanting to make money or to be financially well off is not bad.

- Setting yourself up to be financially well off doesn't happen through luck but rather is something that is learned and worked at.

- Money can be a complex subject; it just takes time to learn just like everything else.

- Learning about investing is important because it allows for your money to work hard for you. To prevent yourself from being overwhelmed, take some time to learn about the different investments out there.

- Managing your money is very important. To get ahead financially, you need to be able to track where you money is going.

- Pay yourself first. Put 10% of your income aside before you spend any of it.

- Debt is something most people don't like to talk about. Being able to manage and pay it off is important. Make sure never to over extend yourself by charging to credit cards things you don't necessarily need. Make sure you always pay your credit cards on time.

- The best investment you can make that will give you the greatest return with no down side is the time you put into educating yourself in the area of finances.

CHAPTER 9:

PURPOSE – THE BIG QUESTION

"If you're walking down the right path and you're willing to
keep walking, eventually you'll make progress."

~ Barack Obama, U.S. President

THE PURPOSE OF LIFE

What is the purpose of life? To be honest, I don't know the definite answer. In school, whenever we spoke about the purpose of life, it was always an abstract "thing." I could never wrap my hands around it. Some of my questions about it were, "How do you find your purpose? When you discover it, how do you know if you are right or wrong?" As a person who likes to have the answers, by not knowing my life's purpose, I drove myself crazy. Since I could not stop until I found the answer to this question, I decided to read books and meet with people I respected and interview them on their thoughts on the purpose of life.

The conclusion I came up with was that a person's purpose in life is something that moves them emotionally. It's something that one is passionate about, and it involves contributing to others in some way or form. For me, I enjoy connecting with people and finding out about their dreams and supporting them to reach it. That excites me. I believe that my purpose in life has to do with working and supporting others in some way or form. You might be thinking, "Well, I have a lot of things I am passionate about and enjoy doing." If so, I know the feeling. I am passionate about several things as well. An important question I asked myself to give me direction was, "Out of all the things you enjoy, which one would you say you like the most or are you more passionate about?" Asking this question helps me to decide which one of my passions ranks the highest.

I also believe no one can tell you what your purpose is. Only you can determine that for yourself.

DON'T WAIT, DECIDE

I recently attended a conference where a top business leader and speaker was talking on the topic of purpose and why many people struggle to find it. He said that many people miss the boat in discovering their purpose because they waste too much time searching to find it, rather than making a decision and choosing their purpose.

This was interesting to hear because this was always counter-intuitive to what I had learned in school about searching for your purpose. He stated that by making a decision about your purpose or what your life is going to be, it helps you to go from having something that is "out there" to something that is real and tangible.

As a junior in high school, I discovered my passion for connecting with people and helping them to achieve their goals and aspirations. I realized my passion was helping others to succeed after I met a speaker who inspired me through his story of helping people with their dreams. I didn't contemplate whether I was making a wrong choice; I just made a decision and worked toward connecting and supporting people. If I were wrong, so be it; at least I was moving in a positive direction.

LIVING YOUR PURPOSE

As a college student, I prided myself for being able to "decide" my purpose pretty early in life. I thought I knew all the answers. I always knew I was passionate about connecting with and helping people. And the way I would do it was through speaking to audiences. After landing my dream job with Tony Robbins, I thought, "I did it. I am living my purpose!" I loved every second of connecting with people and coaching them through challenges, but when I wasn't speaking in front of a group, I felt I wasn't making a difference or living my purpose. I was confused. I thought I had this whole life purpose thing figured out. As I contemplated what I was missing or what I did wrong, I came across a quote that made me say, "Ah, ha!"

> *"The purpose of life is to live a life of purpose."*
> *~ Richard Leider, Counselor and Author*

This quote helped me to understand a mistake I was making and a mistake I find others make as well. As I learned more about purpose, I realized I had always thought one's purpose is a particular thing you do, in my case connecting with people through my talks and seminars. What this quote made me realize was that living your purpose is not a particular thing you do, but rather something you do every single day. In school, I learned how to create long and complicated mission statements, and if I were to strip away the fancy words and boil it all down to the essence of what I do and what I am about, it is caring for other people and believing in them when others don't. Once I made this shift, then living my purpose was no longer just one particular thing I did like speaking to audiences around the world, but something I could do daily, such as simply caring and believing in other people who I come across throughout a day.

YOU MAKE A DIFFERENCE EVERYDAY

Do you believe that once you achieve a particular goal or reach a certain level of success in your life, that you will make a difference? If so, I am here to disagree with you. I believe you make a difference in this world and an impact on other people each and every day whether you know it or not.

The following story was first published in *Chicken Soup for the Soul* and was made into a television movie that aired nationwide on PAX TV. It provides an example of the difference we each make.

WHO I AM MAKES A DIFFERENCE™

By: Helice "Sparky" Bridges

A teacher in New York decided to honor each of her high school seniors for the difference they made in her life. Then she presented each of them with a Blue Ribbon imprinted with gold letters, which read, "Who I Am Makes a Difference."

Afterwards the teacher gave each of the students three more ribbons to acknowledge others, to see what impact it would have in their community. They were to follow up on the results, see who honored whom and report back to the class the following week.

One of the students honored a junior executive in a nearby company for helping him with his career planning. The student gave him a blue ribbon and put it on his shirt just over his heart. Then the boy gave him two extra ribbons, explained their class project on acknowledgement and enlisted the executive's help.

Later that day the junior executive went in to his boss and told him that he deeply admired him for being a creative genius. The junior executive asked him if he would accept the gift of the blue ribbon and would he give him permission to put it on him. His surprised boss said, "Well, sure." After placing the ribbon above his boss' heart, he asked him to support the efforts of the class project and pass on the extra ribbon.

That night the grouchy boss went home to his 14-year-old son and sat him down. He said, "The most incredible thing happened to me today. I was in my office and one of the junior executives came in and told me he admired me and gave me this blue ribbon for being a creative genius. Imagine. He thinks I'm a creative genius. Then he put this blue ribbon that says 'Who I Am Makes a Difference™' on my jacket above my heart. Next he gave me an extra ribbon and asked me to find somebody else to honor. As I was driving home tonight, I started thinking about whom I would honor with this ribbon and I thought about you, son. I want to honor you."

"My days are really hectic and when I come home I don't pay a lot of attention to you. Sometimes I scream at you for not getting good enough grades in school or for your bedroom being a mess. But somehow tonight, I just wanted to sit here and, well, just let you know that you do make a difference to me. Besides your mother, you are the most important person in my life. You're a great kid and I love you!"

The startled boy started to sob and sob, and he couldn't stop crying. His whole body shook. He walked over to a drawer, pulled out a gun, stared at his father and, through his tears said, "I was planning on committing suicide tomorrow, Dad, because I didn't think you loved me. Now I don't need to."

Copyright © 1988 Helice Bridges. Please share this story with everyone you know... Imagine a Blue Ribbon on Every Heart!

It's easy to believe that we have to do something large and extravagant to make a difference in this world. We forget that simple gestures such as a smile or actions like saying, "I appreciate you" to a friend or acquaintance can make a difference in their lives. Even though you may not see the impact on another person, just realize that you make an impact. It's like throwing a rock in a pond. You could leave a ripple effect on that person's life which you will never see, just like the ripple effect that the teacher had in saving that boy's life.

TURNING KNOWLEDGE INTO ACTION

1. What are you passionate about in life? Do you enjoy mentoring others? Do you like working with youths? Take a moment and list your passions.

_____

_____

_____

2. You may not know what your purpose is in life, but that's okay. Let's make a decision and decide what your purpose can be right in this moment. If it changes later on, that's perfectly fine. Make sure that what you write down is something you can do every day. My example is that my purpose is to care for others out of my genuine heart and to believe in them when no else does.

_____

_____

_____

3. In what ways can you live your purpose daily? Is it lending an ear to a friend who is having a difficult time? Maybe it's simply sharing a smile with someone who seems to be having a tough day. Write down three things you can do on a daily basis. Begin to do them today.

_____

_____

_____

TAKE-AWAYS

- No one can tell you what your purpose is; only you will know.

- Don't wait to discover your purpose; decide what your purpose is and what your life will be about.

- One's purpose in life is not a specific thing that you do, but rather something that you can do everyday.

- You make a difference every single day whether you think you do or not. Realize that your actions impact people in ways you would never imagine.

FINAL THOUGHTS

As I finish writing this book, I would have to say it has easily been one of the most difficult things I have ever done in my life. If you knew me, you would know that I hate writing. (I was the student who would struggle to muster out an eight-page term paper; my good friends will attest to that). There were many times throughout this process where I was discouraged, frustrated and wanted to quit. What kept me going was the belief that this book would in some way help you in your life.

I hope that through the stories I shared and the points I made, you feel more prepared and encouraged for what lies ahead in the real world. There will be times in life where you will feel discouraged and overwhelmed; I just want to remind you that everything will be okay. Just remain focused on where you are going and what is important to you. Choose a good group of people to be around you when you are going through tough times.

As you embark on this next phase of your life, I want to wish you the best. Remember that you are not going through this journey alone. I believe in you.

Your Friend,

Hoan Do

Hoan Do

ABOUT THE AUTHOR

Raised by poor immigrant parents who nearly lost their lives to escape the Vietnamese War to come to America, Hoan Do understood at a young age the importance of sacrifice and hard work.

After being accepted to Pepperdine University in Malibu, California, Hoan concentrated on succeeding so he could in return take care of his parents.

With the tremendous pressure Hoan placed on himself, in addition to the stresses of being a college student and frustration about how college wasn't providing him all the tools he needed to succeed in the real world, he felt overwhelmed with anxiety and confusion. With his self-esteem at an all time low, Hoan found himself hitting rock bottom. Refusing to settle and give up, Hoan used this experience as a turning point in his life. He dedicated the rest of his college career to developing the life skills necessary to create balanced success in school and in life.

Immediately after graduating from college, Hoan worked with world-renowned speaker and success coach Tony Robbins. As a national speaker and corporate trainer, Hoan conducted training sessions for distinguished audiences including Coldwell Banker, Century 21, Countrywide, UBS Financial, Toyota, Honda, Washington Mutual, Mary Kay, chambers of commerce all over the United States, and for the U.S. Army.

Today at the age of twenty-three, Hoan owns two companies, is an accomplished author, and an in demand speaker across the country. Recognized as America's College Success Coach, Hoan inspires students worldwide through speaking engagements, coaching programs and his highly acclaimed book, Succeeding in the Real World: What School WON'T Teach You. His mission is to equip young adults with practical and straight-forward advice and knowledge that will help them to succeed in life and in the real world.

HOAN'S FAVORITES

Below is a collection of books and audio CD's that I read or listened to while in school and after graduating that taught me the practical advice and knowledge to succeed in the real world.

Creating Your Own Destiny by Patrick Snow (Success and Goals)

Get the Edge by Tony Robbins (audio program, Life – attitude, goals, health, finances, purpose, you name it, it's in here)

How to Win Friends and Influence People by Dale Carnegie (Communication and Relationships)

Never Eat Alone by Keith Ferrazzi (Business and Relationships)

Rich Dad, Poor Dad by Robert Kiyosaki (Personal Finances)

Secrets of a Millionaire Mind by T. Harv Eker (Personal Finances and Attitude)

The Alchemist by Paulo Coelho (Inspirational and Purpose)

The Magic of Thinking Big by David J. Schwartz (Success and Attitude)

The Monk Who Sold His Ferrari by Robin Sharma (Inspirational, Success and Purpose)

The Present by Spencer Johnson (Attitude)

The Secret by Rhonda Byrne (Success and Attitude)

Think and Grow Rich by Napoleon Hill (Success)

SPEAKING ENGAGEMENTS

When Hoan Do speaks, you can expect a message that creates an instant impact with lasting results.

Hoan Do brings a refreshing approach when speaking to college students. All of his programs are fun and interactive so that students will be engaged and the advice is practical so students will receive information they can take away to use in their lives.

As a recent college graduate, Hoan understands what students are going through and the concerns they have. Through his real world experience, he shares his valuable insights that help students to succeed in school and in life.

BRING HOAN IN TO SPEAK AT YOUR NEXT:

- Leadership Retreat
- Career Day
- Greek/Panhellenic Event
- Conference Keynote and Workshop
- Student Government Program
- Student Orientation

To book Hoan Do for your next event, please contact us at
hoan@succeedingintherealworld.com